BRiSA
THERAPEUTICS

FEELINGS COMPASS

BY TONI SANDS M.ED., LPC, CIT
EMDRIA CERTIFIED EMDR THERAPIST
&
JACQUE BOW ROUSSELOW M.ED., LPC, LCDC,
EMDRIA APPROVED CONSULTANT

The opinions expressed by the Author are not necessarily those held by the Publishers.

The information contained within this book is strictly for informational purposes. The material may include information, products, or services by third parties. As such, the Author and Publisher do not assume responsibility or liability for any third-party material or opinions. The publisher is not responsible for websites (or their content) that are not owned by the publisher. Readers are advised to do their own due diligence when it comes to making decisions.

Published by Franklin Publishers

Printed in the United States of America

For permissions, inquiries, or additional copies, contact:

Franklin Publishers

www.franklinpublishers.com

Website Qr Code

BRISA THERAPEUTICS

FEELINGS C⬦MPASS

A tool to help you efficiently navigate
emotions and get the most out of the
Brisa 'Feel Better in a Breeze' series.

How to use the Brisa Feelings Compass?

Keep Your Compass Handy

Carry the deck with you or place it somewhere accessible during your day. Have the Brisa "Feel Better in a Breeze" series (Volumes 1-4) and your Brisa Journal nearby for deeper exploration.

Pause and Identify Your Emotion

When a strong emotion arises, take a moment to pause. Shuffle through the deck to find the card that best matches how you're feeling.

Flip the Card for Guidance

On the back of the card, you'll find suggested chapters or toolkits from the Brisa books to help process that emotion. These suggestions are tailored to help you feel supported and grounded.

Follow the Suggested Steps

Open the recommended chapter in the Brisa books and try one or more of the exercises. Follow up with a related prompt in your Brisa Journal for deeper reflection.

Explore Additonal Support

For therapist-led exercises or guided audio versions, download the Brisa Therapeutics app from Apple Connect or Google Play. You can also check out The Brisa Courses for more resources.

Take it Step by Step

Healing is a process. Use the Emotions Compass as often as you need to navigate your feelings and rediscover balance.

PAIN

Pause.
Notice where it hurts.
Give yourself permission to feel it.

REST
AND REWIRE

UNPAIN THE BRAIN

Shifts your experience of pain by easing tension and restoring comfort.

OVER WHELMED

Breathe.
Start with one small step.
You don't have to do it all at once.

CALM
IN A BREEZE

INTERNAL RETREAT

Guides users through creating
an emotional sanctuary to alleviate
feelings of overwhelm.

ANXIOUS

Feel your feet on the ground,
take a slow breath, and remind yourself—You're Okay.

CALM
IN A BREEZE

NATURE'S TREASURES

Helps you ground yourself through nature, using the elements to find calm and presence.

WORRIED

Ask yourself:
What can I let go of in this moment?

FLOW
LIKE A RIVER

Chapter Reference

PAPER BOATS

Encourages you to let go of worries by setting them adrift.

INFLAMED

Pause and cool down.
Drink water, breathe slowly, and rest.

Book Reference

FLOW
LIKE A RIVER

Chapter Reference

A RIVER FLOWS

Uses the metaphor of water for relieving tension and inflammation.

REGRETFUL

What's one small way you can show yourself kindness today?

FLOW
LIKE A RIVER

RIDE THE WAVE

Explores letting go of regret and processing
emotions with mindfulness techniques.

STRESSED

Drop your shoulders and exhale slowly.
Let your body soften.

GROW
FROM WITHIN

Chapter Reference

BECOMING

Shapes your future by aligning thoughts, actions, and emotions.

IRRITTABLE

Pause.
Take a deep breath.
Step away for a moment to reset.

GROW
FROM WITHIN

BECOMING

Supports you in shifting frustration into intentional action and growth.

TRIGGERED

Feel your feet on the ground.
Notice three things around you.

FLOW
LIKE A RIVER

Chapter Reference

RIDE THE WAVE

Guides grounding techniques
for emotional triggers.

DOWN

It's okay to rest.
Take one small step when you're ready.

GROW
FROM WITHIN

BECOMING

Encourages you to rise from setbacks, realign with your goals, and move forward with intention.

SAD

Let yourself feel it.
You don't have to carry this alone.

GROW
FROM WITHIN

INNER PARTS

Offers tools to address sadness
with compassion.

STUCK

Ask yourself:
What's one small thing I can do right now?

GROW
FROM WITHIN

INNER PARTS

Provides exercises to unlock
inner strength and overcome stagnation.

INEPT

You are enough.
Name one thing you've done well recently.

GROW
FROM WITHIN

BECOMING

Invites you to reclaim your strengths and step into your potential.

ANGRY

Pause before you react.
Breathe.
Let the feeling settle before you
decide what to do.

GROW
FROM WITHIN

INNER PARTS

Guides users to transform anger
into productive emotions.

BLAH

It's okay to feel off.
Notice one small thing that makes
you feel alive.

REST
AND REWIRE

Chapter Reference

ENERGY RESTORATION

Exercises to overcome
listlessness and regain focus.

SCATTERED

Focus on one thing in front of you.
Start there.

REST
AND REWIRE

ENERGY RESTORATION

Techniques for finding clarity
amidst chaos.

SPACED OUT

Feel the ground beneath you.
Press your feet down and breathe.

CALM
IN A BREEZE

NATURE'S TREASURES

Brings you back to the present by connecting with the elements around you.

TIRED

Close your eyes for a moment.
Rest is a form of strength.

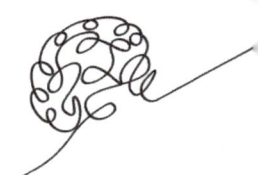

REST
AND REWIRE

ENERGY RESTORATION

Focuses on replenishing physical
and emotional energy.

EXHAUSTED

Do less.
Choose what matters most
and let the rest go.

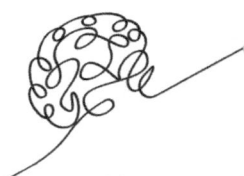

REST
AND REWIRE

ENERGY RESTORATION

Describes methods to
restore energy lost to exhaustion.

FOGGY

Drink water and stretch your body.
Take things one step at a time.

CALM
IN A BREEZE

NATURE'S TREASURES

Clears mental haze by grounding you in the natural world.

HOPEFUL

Hold onto this feeling.
Take one small action to move forward.

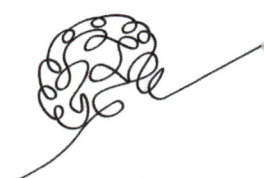

REST
AND REWIRE

SOUL SPA

Inspires feelings of hope and empowerment through mindfulness exercises.

JOYFUL

Let yourself fully enjoy this moment. Happiness deserves space, too.

GROW
FROM WITHIN

VIBING

Amplifies your feel-good energy and deepens your awareness of joy.

READY

Trust yourself.
Take the next step when you're ready.

GROW
FROM WITHIN

VIBING

Aligns your energy with action, preparing you for what's ahead.

INSPIRED

Write it down.
Let your ideas guide your next move.

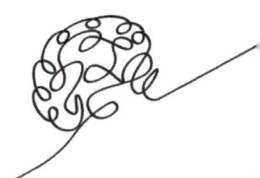

REST
AND REWIRE

SOUL SPA

Exercises to harness
creativity and motivation.

CRAVING

Pause and ask:
What am I really needing right now?

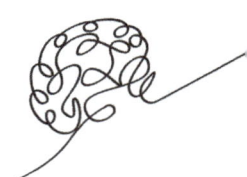

REST
AND REWIRE

ADDICTIVE BEHAVIORS

Guides you in shifting from impulsive urges to mindful choices.

EXCITED

Use this energy for something meaningful. What will you start now?

GROW
FROM WITHIN

VIBING

Taps into your enthusiasm and fuels your momentum forward.

CONTENT

Let yourself fully be in this moment.
You don't need to do or fix anything.

GROW
FROM WITHIN

VIBING

Anchors you in gratitude and appreciation for the present moment.

CAPABLE

Remember:
You've done hard things before.
You can do this too.

GROW
FROM WITHIN

VIBING

Strengthens your belief in yourself and your ability to navigate life.

POSITIVE

Share your light.
Let your optimism ripple outward.

GROW
FROM WITHIN

SOUL SPA

Refreshes your mind and spirit, helping you radiate uplifting energy.

EMPOWERED

Stand tall.
You are stronger than you think.

Book Reference

GROW
FROM WITHIN

Chapter Reference

VIBING

Reconnects you with your inner strength and confidence.

Website Qr Code

Disclaimer

This publication does not provide any medical advice, diagnosis or treatment. The content of this publication is for educational and informational purposes only. The creators are Licensed Professional Counselors and acting as educators in this environment and are not medical doctors. You should always check with a medical professional about any medical issues or symptoms you may be experiencing and before undergoing any new wellness regimen. This publication is not meant to take the place of medical or mental health professional advice. If you are experiencing any type of emergency, please call 911 or go to your nearest medical facility. Never disregard medical advice because of something you read or hear in this publication.

To learn more or find an EMDR therapist go to:

www.emdria.org

-Brisa Therapeutics Founders

Links for information

https://www.springerpub.com/eye-movement-desensitization-and-reprocessing-emdr-scripted-protocols-9780826122391.html

https://www.tandfonline.com/doi/full/10.1080/16506073.2019.1703801?src=recsys#d1e193

https://www.ncbi.nlm.nih.gov/pmc/articles/PMC7716072/

ABOUT THE AUTHOR

Jacqueline Rousselow

Toni Sands

Jacque and Toni are Licensed Professional Counselors and EMDR Certified Therapists. At the time of this publication, they have a combined 25 years of experience as therapists. They co-founded Brisa Therapeutics, an interactive mental health and wellness app and book series in 2021.

Jacque and Toni share a deep life long friendship, as well as the mission to help bring healing and joy to the world. Both Jacque and Toni have a true love for the desert, where they raise their families. They share the passion of learning, teaching and helping others heal.